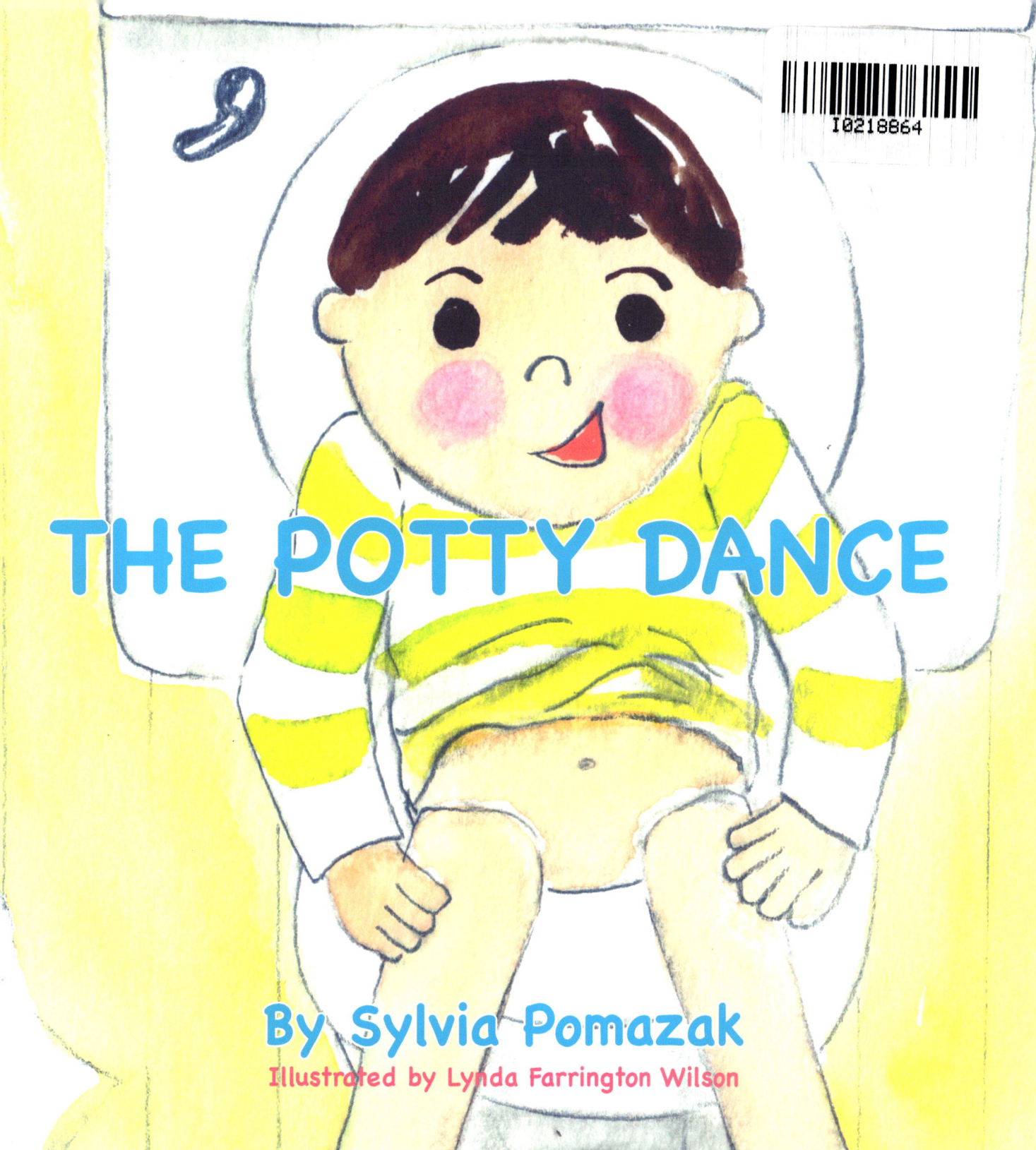

The Potty Dance

© 2014 Sylvia Pomazak

Illustrated by Lynda Farrington Wilson

www.lyndafarringtonwilson.com

All rights reserved.

No part of this book may be reproduced in any matter whatsoever without the written permission of Sylvia Pomazak, except in the case of brief quotations embodied in reviews.

ISBN-10:069225238X
ISBN-13:978-0-692-25238-3

DEDICATION

I would like to thank the following:

My loving and kind husband, Nick, who makes me laugh everyday and is a wonderful father to his boys

My son, Maxton, whose energy and passion keeps me on my toes

My son, Griffin, whose sweetness and gentleness warms my heart

You all fill my life with love and happiness.

Hi there little one.
Are you ready for this?
It's a fun little dance,
That you won't want to miss.

It starts with a seat,
That's really neat.
It's called the potty
where you go poop and pee.

First thing in the morning, you put on underwear.
Then brush your teeth and comb your hair.

Next, it's time for breakfast, that's where we eat.
After you're done, let's try to poop and pee.

Now go to the bathroom as fast as you can,
You can ask your mommy to give you a hand.
Climb up on the potty and take a seat,
Use the step stool or dangle your feet.

Yay, you did it!
The pee pee's coming out.
It's time to celebrate, get up, twist and shout.

Pull up your pants and make sure you flush,
Take your time, there's no reason to rush.

Now step up to the sink,
And wash your hands.
When you're all done, you can do
the potty dance.

Put your hands up and wave
them in the air,
Twist and shout for all to hear.

Now it's time to go and start to play.
You can use the potty throughout the day.

If you feel the pee or poop
is starting to come out,
Just jump right up, raise your hands
and give a loud shout,

"I have to make pee, I have to go poop"
Then run to the potty, it's all up to you.

After you practice for a couple of days,
It will become easier in so my ways.
You may have an accident
And that's okay,
Just keep on trying everyday.

Before you know it you will start to stay dry,
And to all those diapers you can say ...

Bye bye.

ABOUT THE AUTHOR

Sylvia Pomazak resides in the suburbs of Chicago with her husband and two boys. She enjoys spending time with her family and watching her boys grow up.

Her book was created out of the joy of reading stories to her kids and watching them learn.

www.ingramcontent.com/pod-product-compliance
Lightning Source LLC
Chambersburg PA
CBHW041233040426
42444CB00002B/150